W9-BEB-733

FAMILIES AROUND THE WORLD

A family from
CHINA

Julia Waterlow

RSVP

RAINTREE
STECK-VAUGHN
PUBLISHERS
The Steck-Vaughn Company

Austin, Texas

FAMILIES AROUND THE WORLD

A family from **BOSNIA**

A family from **BRAZIL**

A family from **CHINA**

A family from **ETHIOPIA**

A family from **GERMANY**

A family from **GUATEMALA**

A family from **IRAQ**

A family from **JAPAN**

A family from **SOUTH AFRICA**

A family from **VIETNAM**

The family featured in this book is an average Chinese family. The Wus have been chosen because they are a typical Chinese family in terms of income, housing, number of children, and lifestyle.

Cover: The Wus outside their home with all their possessions
Title page: Jian Chun and Rong wash clothes outside their home.
Contents page: Two women cycle to work.

Picture Acknowledgments: All the photographs in this book were taken by Leong Ka Tai. The photographs were supplied by Material World/Impact Photos and were first published in 1994 by Sierra Club Books in *Material World: A Global Family Portrait* © Copyright Peter Menzel/Material World. The map artwork on page 4 was produced by Peter Bull.

© Copyright 1998, text, Steck-Vaughn Company

Published by Raintree Steck-Vaughn Publishers, an imprint of Steck-Vaughn Company

Printed in Italy. Bound in the United States.
1 2 3 4 5 6 7 8 9 0 02 01 00 99 98

Library of Congress Cataloging-in-Publication Data
Waterlow, Julia.
A family from china / Julia Waterlow.
p. cm.—(Families around the world)
Includes bibliographical references and index.
Summary: Describes the activities of a family of farmers living in southern China, providing brief information about daily life and customs.
ISBN 0-8172-4912-5
1. Family—China—Juvenile literature.
2. China—Social life and customs—Juvenile literature.
[1.Family life—China. 2. China—Social life and customs.]
I. Title. II. Series: Families around the world.
HQ684.W38 1998
306.85'0951—dc21 97-41243

Contents

Introduction

China is the third largest country in the world.

CHINA

Capital city:	Beijing
Size:	3,705,000 sq. mi. (9,597,000 sq. km)
Number of people:	1,251,000,000
Language:	Mainly Mandarin Chinese
People:	93 percent are Chinese.
Religion:	Not many Chinese are religious. Some are Buddhists. A few people are Muslims or Christians.
Currency:	Yuan

THE WU FAMILY

Size of household:	9 people
Size of home:	1,185 sq. ft. (110 sq. m)
Workweek:	60 hours at busy times of year (adults)
Most valued possessions:	Ba Jiu: Television Dong: Bicycle
Family income:	$3,300 each year

The Wus are an ordinary Chinese family. They have put everything they own outside their home so that this photograph could be taken.

Meet the Wu Family

1 Ba Jiu, father, 59
2 Yu Xian, mother, 57
3 Wen De, elder son, 30
4 Jian Chun, his wife, 28
5 Dong, their son, 8

6 Xi, their daughter, 3
7 Wen Bin, second son, 25
8 Rong, his wife, 25
9 Xue, their daughter, 3

A CROWDED COUNTRY

More people live in China than in any other country in the world. Because China is very crowded, most families are only allowed to have one child. In rural areas, families are allowed to have two children.

Ba Jiu and Yu Xian live with their sons, who are grown up and have families of their own. Their elder son, Wen De, has a wife and two children. Their younger son, Wen Bin, is also married. He has one daughter. Ba Jiu and Yu Xian are very happy to have their children and grandchildren living with them.

"We are allowed to have two children. We hope our second child will be a boy."—*Rong*

The Wu House

The Wus live in a traditional Chinese house. It has curved roofs and is built around a courtyard. In front of the house there is a big fish pond.

TOWN AND COUNTRY

Most people in China still live in towns or villages in the countryside. They usually have more space in their houses than the Chinese who live in cities. China's cities are very crowded. Many people live in tiny spaces, with just one or two rooms.

A Country Home

The Wus are farmers who live in southern China. Their house is in the countryside. It takes them fifteen minutes to walk to the nearest village, which is called Shiping.

Inside the Wus' house there is a living room, a kitchen, and three bedrooms. There are several storerooms as well. There, the Wus keep tools, food, bits of wood, and even old newspapers and boxes. Ba Jiu doesn't like to throw useful things away. Outside, there is also a sheltered area, where the Wus keep their pigs.

"I'm used to doing the washing by hand, but it would be nice to have a washing machine."—*Jian Chun*

There is no faucet inside the house, so the family collects water every day from a nearby well. Rong and Jian Chun usually do the washing in a pool beside the house.

"We like to watch television together in the evenings."—*Ba Jiu*

Old and New

Ba Jiu and Yu Xian like the old furniture in the living room. The rest of the family prefers modern furniture, so Wen De and Wen Bin have bought some new chairs. One thing that everyone likes is the color television. It is in the middle of the room so everyone can watch it easily.

Hot Summers

In the summer it gets very hot, so the Wus have electric fans in each room. When it gets too warm, they switch on the fans to keep the rooms cool. The Wus all have net curtains around their beds. They pull the curtains around at night so that mosquitoes can't bite them while they are asleep.

Dong keeps his toys in a drawer in his parents' bedroom.

Food and Cooking

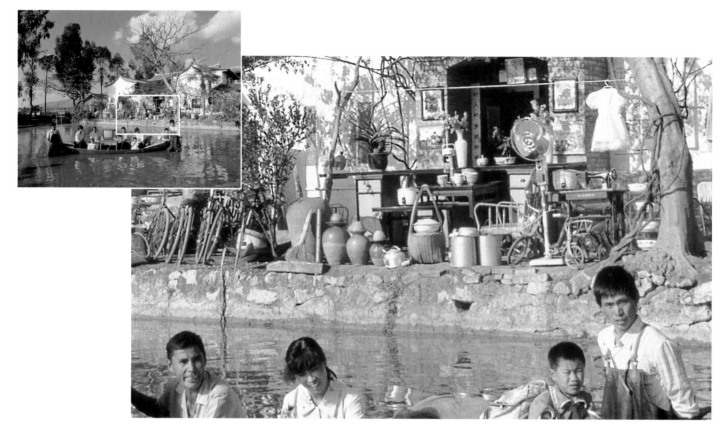

The Wus store dried and pickled food in jars and baskets.

RICE AND NOODLES

The Chinese eat either rice or noodles with their meals. People in southern China mostly eat rice, and people in northern China mostly eat noodles. Rice grows best in the south, where the weather is warmer and wetter.

Storing Food

The Wus grow most of their food themselves. They dry or pickle food such as cabbage, beans, and fish and put the food in big jars. This way, they can keep it for several months and it will still be good to eat.

Rice With Everything

The Wus eat rice with every meal. For breakfast they have a kind of sticky rice, and the children drink soya milk, which is made from a type of bean. For lunch and supper everyone eats rice with vegetables. Sometimes the family has fish. They don't eat meat very often because it is too expensive.

Wen De spoons his breakfast into a small bowl. The Wus eat their food with chopsticks.

Fast Food

Yu Xian likes to prepare the food for special meals, when the whole family eats together. First, she chops the food into small pieces. This is so the food cooks quickly, and she doesn't have to use too much fuel. She fries or boils most of the food in a big wok. Yu Xian saves time by using an electric steamer to cook the rice.

This big pan is called a wok. Yu Xian is making soup in it.

"I prepare the food for my family sometimes. They all say I'm a great cook!"—*Wen De*

The Wus at Work

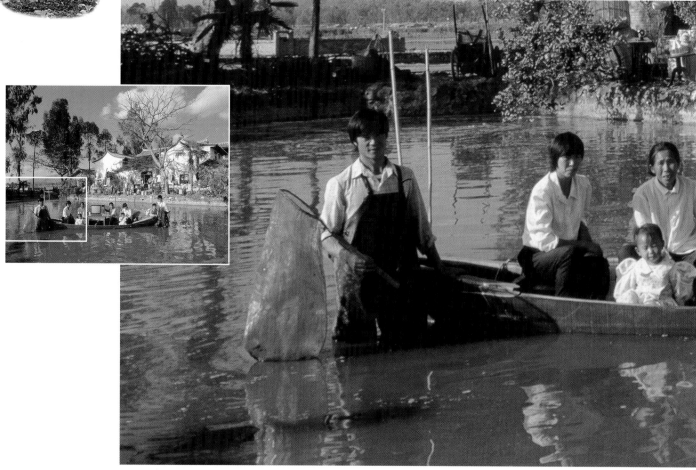

The Wus grow vegetables and keep fish. Wen Bin wears plastic overalls so he can wade into the pond to catch the fish.

In China, most women work and look after their family. Many Chinese people still work in the countryside as farmers. Often, young people move to cities, where they hope they will find better-paid jobs.

Fishing Folk

The pond in front of the Wus' house is full of fish. The Wus share the pond with their neighbors. Wen De and Wen Bin feed the fish until they are big enough to eat. Then they catch and sell them.

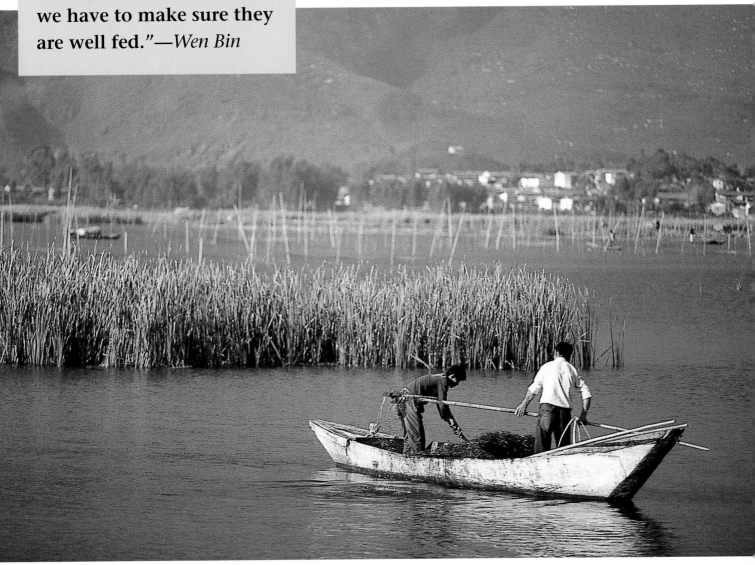

"We can make a lot of money from our fish, so we have to make sure they are well fed."—*Wen Bin*

Taking care of the fish is hard work. Every few days, Wen De and Wen Bin take their boat to Jade Dragon Lake. There, they collect weeds that the fish like to eat. The fish are valuable, so the Wus and their neighbors guard the pond at night. Otherwise, thieves might come and steal the fish. The Wus have been lucky—no one has stolen any fish yet.

Wen De and Wen Bin collect weed from Jade Dragon Lake.

Everyday Work

The Wus always have plenty of jobs to do. Wen De and Wen Bin look after the fish. Rong and Jian Chun take care of the pigs. They do the housework, such as washing and cleaning, as well. Yu Xian and Ba Jiu help by looking after their grandchildren while everyone else is busy.

The Wus have planted orange trees. Wen De is starting to pick the ripe fruit.

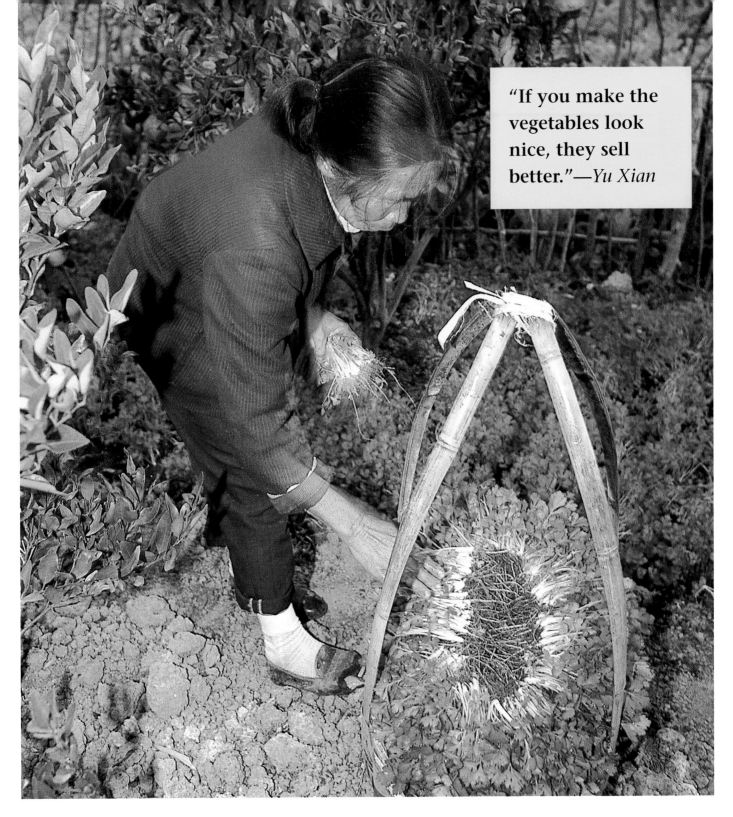

"If you make the vegetables look nice, they sell better."—*Yu Xian*

The Wus grow all kinds of vegetables to sell at the market. Their onions and cabbages are especially good. Everyone helps in the fields, planting, watering, hoeing, and picking. The Wus have to do all the work by hand.

Busy Times

Yu Xian and Ba Jiu carry their vegetables to market in bamboo baskets.

The Wus are very busy at certain times of the year. The busiest times are when the fish are ready for market and when the vegetables and rice have to be planted and harvested. Then, everyone works from sunrise to sunset. Even Dong, who is only eight, has to help.

Sunday is market day in Shiping. Yu Xian and Ba Jiu leave early to take the vegetables to the market. Ba Jiu always sells the vegetables himself.

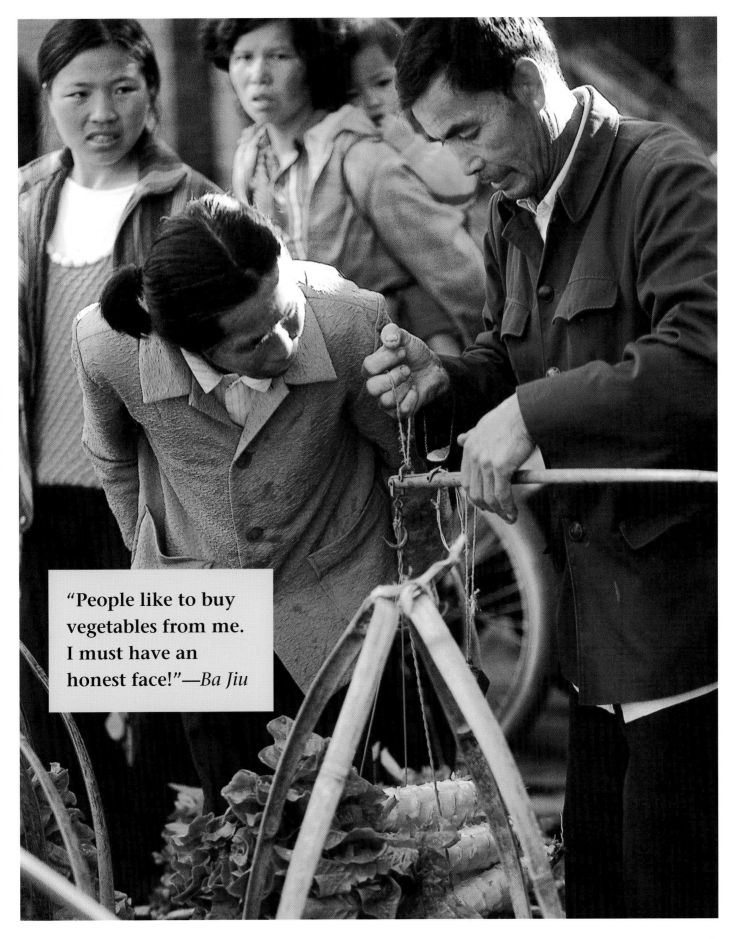

"People like to buy vegetables from me. I must have an honest face!"—*Ba Jiu*

School and Play

Wen De's son, Dong, goes to the local school in Shiping.

There is no alphabet in Chinese. Instead, each word is written as a "character," like the ones on the wall in the picture at the top of page 23. Chinese children have to learn thousands of characters by heart when they are beginning to read and write.

Off To School

It is still dark when Dong gets up to go to school. After a quick breakfast, he dashes off to reach his school in Shiping by half-past seven. He is usually late and has to run most of the way. Dong comes home every day to have his lunch.

Dong learns math and Chinese. Dong's classroom is very plain. The school does not have much money for furniture and equipment. During breaks, his class exercises on the playground.

Dong's classmates outside their school

Dong and his friends exercise every day.

> "I like school, but playing with my friends is more fun!" —*Dong*

Dong and his friends rush out of school at the end of the day.

Time To Play

Dong is full of energy. When he gets back from school, he rushes around the house, pretending to be an airplane. Dong's grandmother is always telling him to be quiet. Sometimes, Dong likes to sit in the living room and read. Kung Fu books and comics are his favorites.

Xi and Xue are too young to go to school. They spend most of their time playing around the house. Sometimes, their mothers take the girls with them to the fields. Xi and Xue play together while their mothers work.

Xi and Xue play in one of the storerooms, where the family keeps baskets of rice.

Spare Time

Everyone in the Wu family loves watching television.

HOLIDAY TIME

The biggest holiday in China is the Chinese New Year. It does not have a fixed date but is usually in January or February. Families get together to eat, drink, and visit relatives and friends. People decorate their houses and set firecrackers off in the streets.

After Work

The Wu family has little spare time. After a hard day's work, they all enjoy sitting down and watching television. The grownups like to watch the news and programs about other places in the world.

Going To Town

The Wus don't have much money to spend on themselves. Jian Chun and Rong share a sewing machine and make their own clothes. Every now and then, they put on their best skirts and blouses and go to town. They like to look at the clothes in the shops there. Sometimes, Jian Chun and Rong go to the hairdresser for a haircut.

Rong and Jian Chun look for bargains at the market.

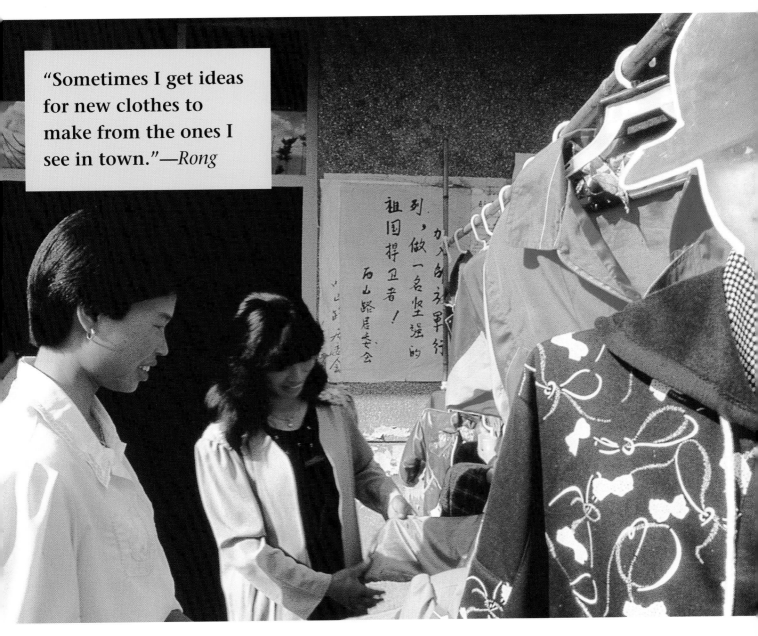

"Sometimes I get ideas for new clothes to make from the ones I see in town."—*Rong*

The Future

Life for ordinary Chinese people is better than ever before. But the population is huge and growing. In the future, one of China's big problems will be making sure that everyone has a home and enough food, water, and electricity.

The Wus are happy with their way of life. They have enough food to eat. They have been able to buy a television, radios, and some new furniture. They would like a video recorder and a refrigerator. Wen Bin thinks they ought to buy better tools for farming and fishing.

Dong likes playing in the fields with his sister and his friends.

28

The Wus work very hard. Every month, they are able to put some money in the bank. They are saving it to help their children as they grow up. The Wus think it is very important to look after their children's future.

Pronunciation Guide

Ba Jiu	Ba-jee-oo	**Wen De**	When-Dee
		Wen Bin	When-Bin
Jian Chun	Jee-en Choon	**Wu**	Woo
Shiping	Shee-peng	**Yu Xian**	Yoo Shee-en
Xue	Shway		
Xi	Shee		

Glossary

Bamboo A very strong plant with a woody stem.

Chopsticks A pair of thin sticks that Chinese people use to pick up their food.

Communists People who belong to the Communist political party. They believe that work and money should be shared equally.

Courtyard An area surrounded by buildings or walls.

Emperor A ruler of a very large area of land.

Firecrackers Small fireworks that make a loud bang when they go off.

Fuel Materials such as wood or coal that are burned on a fire.

Kung Fu A Chinese sport.

Mosquitoes Small insects that bite. The bites are very itchy.

Noodles A dried food, made from flour.

Pickle To put food in salty water or vinegar, to keep it from going bad.

Population The number of people who live in a country.

Traditional Something that has been done in a certain way for a very long time.

Books to Read

Dawson, Imogen. *China* (Postcards from). Austin, TX: Raintree Steck-Vaughn, 1995.

James, Ian. *China* (Inside). Danbury, CT: Franklin Watts, 1989.

Tan, Jennifer. *Food in China* (International Food Library). Vero Beach, FL: Rourke Corp., 1989.

Terzi, Marinella. *The Chinese Empire* (World Heritage). Danbury, CT: Children's Press, 1992.

Waterlow, Julia. *China: City and Village Life* (Country Insights). Austin, TX: Raintree Steck-Vaughn, 1997.

Index